Coming Back Home

Coming Back Home

Poems On Leaving Prison

EDITED BY
N. THOMAS JOHNSON-MEDLAND

RESOURCE *Publications* • Eugene, Oregon

COMING BACK HOME
Poems On Leaving Prison

Copyright © 2018 N. Thomas Johnson-Medland. All rights reserved. Except for brief quotations in critical publications or reviews, no part of this book may be reproduced in any manner without prior written permission from the publisher. Write: Permissions, Wipf and Stock Publishers, 199 W. 8th Ave., Suite 3, Eugene, OR 97401.

Resource Publications
An Imprint of Wipf and Stock Publishers
199 W. 8th Ave., Suite 3
Eugene, OR 97401

www.wipfandstock.com

PAPERBACK ISBN: 978-1-5326-1954-0
HARDCOVER ISBN: 978-1-4982-4589-0
EBOOK ISBN: 978-1-4982-4588-3

Manufactured in the U.S.A.

Dedicated to all them that have awakened and realized that setting ourselves free is the goal. And, to them that have taken to putting down in words, the path to that awakening.

"Our future depends upon our appreciation of the reality of the inner life, of the splendor of thought, of the dignity of wonder and reverence. This is the most important thought: God has a stake in the life of man, of every man. But this idea cannot be imposed from without; it must be discovered by every man; it cannot be preached, it must be experienced."

—Abraham Joshua Heschel, Insecurity of Freedom: Essays on Human Existence

"Why do you stay in prison, when the door is so wide open?"

—Jalaluddin Mevlana Rumi

INTRODUCTION

IF YOU HAVE NEVER been inside of a prison, there are things you will not know about the community there. You may guess at them, but that is not the same. What it feels like. What it sounds like. What goes on there; these all define portions of what it is. These definitions, or parameters of life inside, come to you quite viscerally. You feel them in and through your skin before you actually give word or shape to understanding them. You sense before you think.

First, there are lots of doors. Each new door lets you further in to the prison. There are layers to life inside of a prison. You come in so far. You stop. You are processed or cleared. Then you can move closer in. Doors close, are locked, you are processed again. Depending on your reason for being there, you will be processed at each layer of the community and allowed into the next place you belong. Doors close, are locked, you are processed again; until you arrive where you belong for why you are there. You go nowhere without a reason or a purpose.

Second, there is an order to life there. You don't exactly know what it is while you are there—while you are VISITING, but from the rooms, the walls, to the clothing, everything means something and you better learn it fast if you want to survive inside. Like the first, impression above, this order is a layering of life. And, it is sensed before it is thought about.

* * *

It took me several weeks before I realized both things were a lot like beehives. There are layers to the beehive, and there is order to the beehive. You can only get into the activity of the hive by passing through a lot of layers and performing amid those layers in a certain way. You cannot get to the panels of comb unless you carry the scent of the hive—the scent of the Queen. You cannot get to the brood unless you are there to work on the brood. To the honey unless you are there to work on the honey. To the Queen, unless you are there to work for the Queen. Purpose and meaning and permission are everywhere in both of these communities.

Another thing about hives is that bees move throughout the assigned jobs based on their age. Each one gets to play most of the roles in the hive before they die. They cannot become Queen or drone after they are born into the hive, but even before they are pupated, they could become any kind of bee—depending on what they are fed and how they are nurtured. Once they are born into the hive the worker bees go through a series of roles based on age.

The worker bees in the hive begin with feeding the older and then the younger larvae. Then they make wax, build comb, carry food, and carry the dead bees out of the hive. They then guard the hive entrance. Finally, the whole last half of their lives (a total of about 45 days) they collect pollen, nectar, and water for the hive and pollinate plants. Very rhythmic and very routine. But, at first blush or first view, you would not know that this was the schedule. You could sense or feel an ordered existence by movement in and through the hive, but on closer, more time based study of the hive, its genius emerges.

After being in the prison hive for a while, you realize that all of life is highly mechanized and routinized like this. The prison seems special at first because it is a contained society. A captivated hive. Outside the walls of the prison; however, there are hundreds and thousands of other hives of life. They may be less contained by walls and wire, but they are there. And, there are even hives in the heart, and the mind, and the soul. Contained and rhythmed ways to live and move and be layered among the other members of whatever hive you are tending or dwelling in. Hives within hives.

* * *

The opening and closing of doors and locking of locks is the subtle backdrop of time ticking away. The pendulum of life inside. For them that come and go with ease—only visiting those who live in the hive—there comes an awakening one day. One day, you hear the door behind you lock as you leave the confines of wall, wire, and hive. You look around you and you

Introduction

realize that as you hurry to your next activity, or place, or hive, that you are really no more free than the "bees" on the "inside". That freedom in and freedom to and freedom from are all simply stages of the work we are about in the GRANDE HIVE. That because the door locks behind you, it does not mean that you are free. And then, you start to hear things that go on inside, with a different ear.

That is really the beginning of the interpretation of incarceration. You would have to peel back hundreds of layers to get at each and every of the many ways it is lived, held, and enforced by, to, and upon them that are on the inside. But, it is just like that on the outside. Thousands of layers to peel back. One of the layers is the confined nature of the majority of the members of the hive. Unlike a beehive, not all of the bees in the hive get to leave the hive and return as a portion of their life's mission. Most of the people in a prison hive stay put. It is only a handful who leave and come back. In this fact, the metaphor clearly breaks down.

But, there is an extension to the image of the prison as hive and the inmates that leave. Those who do come back to the prison hive, are all the more elevated in stature for having done so. There is a gaining of status at the return.

It was in this hive that we sought to study and write poems.

* * *

The conversations we had would start around the poets we were reading. We read Frost, Stafford, and Bly for the Modern American Male Poets classes. Then Oliver, Rich, and Shihab Nye for the Modern American Female Poets classes. I had saved Neruda for the final series. Each of the series were three weeks long. I taught each three-week series three times. This enabled us to get it offered for each of the cell blocks in the prison. The sessions went from having one student to having fourteen. It varied week to week.

After reading and discussing and sharing hunches on what these poets were trying to portray, we would stop and write poems. Simple exercises would start with instructions like: "pick something you love, write down a bunch of words that describe that thing you love, and then we will talk about it." Always, folks needed another prompt. So, I would say, "write about a favorite place that you love to go, or a favorite memory that you think about often." That was usually enough to get the writer engine started. And then, the magic would begin. We would say, "Let's go back and add some colors to your poem. Or, some emotions. Or, some sounds." And so, the poems would grow.

* * *

Like it or not, just about everything is traceable back to physics. It all gets down to SPACE and or TIME. Talk about places and that is space. Talk about memories, that is space in time. Talk about people and they are beings in both space and time. Space and time tend to divide everything up into atomistic and bite-sized hunks and chunks that we recognize and can assign to some sort of order in the physical universe and in our minds. And so, these little vignettes that prisoners would begin to write would begin a process for them in unfolding their understanding of space and time. Their space; and their time. Who and how they were in the universe of things.

It didn't take too many reminders to get them to add color, aroma, taste, feel, texture, sounds, impressions, and all the other words that help to give description some dimension in space and time. Filling things out and making them more solid—more real—was easy. And, the prisoners would help each other. Suggestions were less likely, but praise was clearly rendered to fellow poets.

Almost every prisoner balked at not having anything. That what they wrote was no good. Not finding any meaning in their first scribbles. But, every one of them wrote. And, when they read their words out loud, they were amazed to find how deep and palpable their images could be. How others could walk around their words and get a view from just the other side of what they had said.

Only one prisoner stopped after reading his first poem and did not read anything else out loud that one night. Do you know what stopped him? Some inside innuendo. Some racial taunt by a member of the class who was insecure about his own order and sound of words. Some meaningless human pandering that was based on one man's lack of confidence in what he wrote. This jab by another, made one man shut down. And, that brought me back to where I was. I saw who was in charge in this piece of the hive. But, out of all my time in the prison, that was the only time that happened. Once. And, one week there was a fight.

I was with other frail and wounded humans who sometimes need to climb up on top of other people to feel taller. While I addressed the taunter's

Introduction

words, and helped him to work with his poem to gain confidence, his one snide remark shutdown the other man for the rest of the class.

I was reminded of the fragility of being human. It is a vulnerable thing to be in space and time. But, it was no different inside these walls than outside of them. The same incident described above happens over and over in groups we belong to all our lives. It isn't just a prison thing. It's a freedom thing. When people don't feel confident in their own freedom, they tend to like to put others behind some sort of bars. It gives them clout. We have all seen our loved ones do it. We have all seen presidents do it, too.

The beauty of art and its creation is that it can open us to the freedom of life and the freedom within. It can add a dimension of dignity and worth; value and capability. It allows those who are about it to give representation to what is unseen; to make solid the invisible and infinitesimal. But, art too is fragile and it often breaks because of other peoples' intrusion into the process too soon. That is how art is so much like life.

* * *

The themes that come from a prison poet are varied. Most poems you would not have to know the poet was a prisoner to gain access to the import of the word-pictures. Human experience while diverse shares some common archetypal qualities. But, some will grow in meaning knowing where the poems were planted. I think themes about being captive are universal, but when you know the poet is in a prison, it can open you to listen differently. Is that a good thing? I don't know. But it is true.

I know that one of the themes we talk about again and again in our weekly poetry class is being a prisoner. Not the most obvious definition of being a prisoner, but the more subtle one. Everyone has prisons in their lives. Sometime each unit, we tend to list out the types of prisons we are all up against as humans. The lists—regardless of which cellblock—are always the same. They are the same because they are archetypal.

People are prisoners to: relationships (good and bad), jobs, social morays, values, beliefs, drugs, cigarettes, addictions, sex, religion, people, depression, anxiety, food, alcohol, body image, and on and on it goes. We all have such potential to passively live our lives in the invisible bars of any of the above. What sets that prison of invisible bonds apart from the one with cell doors and locks is that you can forget you are a prisoner. In a jail, there is no forgetting. From sight, to sound, and every other sense, there is no forgetting where you are—for very long that is—when you are in a jail.

On the outside we speak about things we constantly rub up against in different terms from those things in life that are just beyond our daily realizations. But, is that any different than in a jail—just without bars?

Monday morning on the outside is one clear moment when we all know we are CAUGHT in a trap. Having just rebuilt your life—over the weekend—with the joy of leisure and cascade of chosen minutia, we slam head-on into having to step back into a work life which remains always just beyond our pleasure points. Even in the best of jobs. A little bit of friction each hour that you can't wait to move beyond.

* * *

Let's look at the themes we have collected from our poets. In our poems we will reach into a tension that exists in all our lives of the "almost, but not yet". It is that time and place in life, where the things we long for and hunger for are just beyond our grasp. It is the place of anticipation, and desire.

We look at shifting family and friend relationships that are altered by the necessity of being apart. We will find hurt and woundedness at being duped by ourselves or someone else. We will unearth whole troves of things missed because of separation: pie, pencils, passion, intimacy, the smell of fires and the pure silence of the heart. Trust. Power. Isolation, punishment, and despair.

Not so very different from the poems we read on the outside. But, there is a slight twisting of the dimensionality of the imagery. It is somehow given a larger dose of longing or desire for its object. There is a clearer line that you can draw from the subject to the object that is just a shade different from another's attempt to reveal the same thing.

Sometimes that clearer line is because we know that the poet is a prisoner (at least in my class and in this volume of poems). But, at other times there is a way of speaking about things, a way of describing things that puts a fuller stop on the idea of fulfillment. We get a sense that what is longed for is genuinely out of reach. Albeit, that may be temporary, but it is nonetheless a full stop—it is out of reach. For now. And, we may not learn from the poet's words, just how long that out-of-reachness will go. The bars tend to dash peoples' abilities to pretend everything is attainable.

Introduction

In these poems, I think you will find a collection of themes which speak to time, space, human ingenuity, and longing. The longing for what is not present in their physical world is like the shadow pain of a Civil War amputee. There is an ongoing sense that one needs to tend and care for something that is no longer present. The students here opened their minds to find their hearts and to write their souls. The students are not merely prisoners of society, but as with the rest of us, often prisoners of themselves—ID, EGO, and SUPEREGO. Prisoners of life and its despair, regret, catharsis, change, hope, pain, anguish, and all that is longed for, desired, and missed.

I am pleased to add a handful of my own poems to the mix; poems written while at the prison or when working on our homework assignments. The themes we were nourished on in our sessions are archetypal and universal and should feed you at many levels.

Student Poems

ODE TO A PEN

RUSSELL

> By yourself, you're nothing.
> Stationery stationary.
> Often discarded,
> mostly overlooked,
> taken for granted,
> forgotten.
> When you're needed, you're God.
> You can create and infinite number of universes
> with a swirl or a flourish.
> You can enact laws,
> declare wars,
> confirm life,
> report death.
> You are mightier than a sword,
> a gun,
> a grenade,
> a bomb.
> In your many forms,
> you witnessed the birth of freedoms,
> the abolishment of bondage,
> of unrighteousness,
> of slavery.
> You are a weapon that can be carried by every living man,
> woman,
> child.
> Yet, you are rarely equipped,
> replaced by technology,
> left in desk drawers,
> unimportant,
> antiquated.

I long for days when you return to your former glory,
edified.
Alas, by yourself, you're nothing,
but without you, so are we, so are we.

FREEDOM OF THOUGHTS

Russell

Freedom is often misinterpreted.
An augmented imagination of what's called "reality".
Time is wasted on fruitless fantasies.
Nothing ventured, nothing gained.
Trying to find the meaning or purpose.
Underneath an intricate, inter-connected lattice-work
Of unattainable dreams and aspirations.
We strive to uncover hidden talents to conform to human acceptance.
Never realizing we incarcerate ourselves in the prison of our peers.
Freedom is most often described as a physical state.
Our feeble minds compensate for the overwhelming world before us.
Where we are right now, physically, is most important.
We forget whether by choice or mistake, that our mind controls our bodies.
We pretend that mind over matter is not a tangible thing.
We accept that these bricks, this steel, this prison is not malleable.
That underneath they are made from the same elements we are.
We are the bricks.
We are the steel.
We are the prison.
One day the gates will open for us all.
Until then, regardless of where you are physically,
The world will always be your prison.
Whether you can see the walls.
Or not.

ARGUMENT

Russell

    Piece by piece, brick by brick,
    We attempt to close this distance between us.
    This chasm has formed, as vast as oceans,
    Unencumbered by the boundaries of land.

    Inch by inch, step by step,
    We mend the wounds that caused us pain.
    We bridge the void of silence,
    Oft with more silence, for words a blade.

    Each statement a piercing projectile,
    Intentionally delivered with fatal precision.
    The deafening thunder crescendos,
    But the ensuing silence is what we hear the clearest.

    When the empty casings of spent remarks litter the ground,
    When the smoke, thick and black and acrid clears,
    When we are at last disarmed and defenseless,
    The screaming echoes of nothing demand to be heard.

    Now as the tumult settles and casualties accounted for,
    We see the only scars we have are self-inflicted.
    By trying to hurt each other, we only harm ourselves,
    Leaving an emptiness, as black as night, in our eyes.

    I reach for you, and you retract,
    The verbal assault constructing physical barriers.
    A ragged canyon spanning what was once common ground,
    And I've never felt so far away than I do now in front of you.

Still, piece by piece, inch by inch,
We suture the frayed and tattered edges, our fragile fabric.
We realize a temporary fissure isn't worth a permanent rift,
Finally, we find our way back—to each other.

CUTS

Russell

Flawless canvas,
smooth and sincere.
The razorblade paintbrush,
long and steady strokes.
A deep red hue,
straight and purposeful.
The Northern light fades,
an unfinished picture.
The artist's muse
darkness eternal.
Art reflects life,
death reflects art.
A picture's value,
1000 words.
The value of life,
unspoken tomes.
Metal to skin,
slashed with a purpose.
All that life is,
scratching the surface.
Never to know,
the depth or the reasons.
The blade's edge,
cold and cunning.
Warm and free,
the red river flows.
Drains to the ocean,
returns to the canvas.

MIND MATTER PARADOX

JOE

As I lay here still,
trapped in a cage
Preparing for the fight outside;
inside I awake and lay here in this cage
for Just this moment,
I broke free, from a cage; to write this poem
I look around now as I lay here, still;
trapped in a cage
preparing for the fight outside
like a continuous paradox
I may break free from Hell
but I'll always remain a prisoner to my mind. . .
. . .inside. . ..

MEAL

Brigham

That smell
wakes me————————————or is it the nurse
delivering good cheer————————and drugs?
My cellmates diabetic test strip
reads 128 this morning;
good job!

The block stirs————————stretching;
waking, belching, coughing, and cursing.
Dope sneezes blows
through lingering dreams,
like a heroin-fueled foghorn warning of
that smell.
That hideous danger hides,
waits——————to sink us all;
this ship of fools.

Breakfast?
No——————————that mess sits
cold
in the sallyport.

Inhaling————it's unmistakable now...
Lunch!

Later,
I pluck a feather from
mechanically
separated
chicken;

that smell.

LAST DAY

Brigham

    The time has come
    to read my will.
    A stranger thing to hear
    with living ear.
    My precious things passing
    to the hands of
    friends?
    Here, where proximity
    and necessity dictate terms——————yes,
    I must call them friends.

    John gets the shaver.
    Kenny scores shampoo (and leftover lotion).
    Jeremiah takes the sugar supply.
    Corey accepts the cache of coffee (freeze dried).
    I leave the radio to Dan.

    Business concluded,
    they thank me, of course,
    for those precious things.
    They promise to write, of course,
    or call.
    None will ever call
    or write,
    and that's fine.
    The lie is gentle————harmless.

Outside the gate,
I kiss my wife;
hug my kids.
I never————ever

waste another thought
on precious
junk.

LOST

Merritt

Lost in the wind
Deprived by sin
Here we only dream of home
And loved ones we left alone
This is where forgotten souls roam
Some come n' go
More than a few has a long way to go
Every day is the same
No one but their selves to blame
Glorified stories, this the price of fame
Now we all share the same décor
From the stone walls to the floor
The metal toilet to the steel door
Life wasn't this empty too long ago
Look how time has flown
All that precious time is gone
Now ask yourself was it worth it
Nothing in this big blue world is perfect
But if you work hard for it
You would think that you deserve it
Everything seems good above the surface
Until you realize the dream you brought
Wasn't worth the purchase

HIMSELF...

Justin

He needs a way to be himself, without being himself, he barely had anyone say they need him, from that point on he never wanted to be himself again, and for the people that talked to him, he didn't even want to see or speak to them, but he couldn't say any of this to them or anyone else, so he just left, for once in his life, he was satisfied, after a long period of time, he evolved, simply to nobody else, but himself without being himself, but now the worst has happened to him, he's now stuck behind brick walls, thinking about his life all over again, he changed his look, his personality, all back to his old self, now he's half-way there, realizing he has to stop the crying because the end is near, and he just needs to get out of here, someone tells him that "it only takes a little bit of faith to move a mountain" but he knows he's only he only got a little bit of faith left, now he's deciding if when he gets out if he either wants to be himself again or the other person he used to be. . ..

OOPS...

Justin

I was outside living life, but something. . . just now moved, through my heart like the sharpest of blades, I feel the cold metal against my wrist till the blood stops flowing, then my heart rate gets slower, my breathing gets deeper, it's like time stopped, all I hear is my heart beating, a tear goes down my face, I feel like a big disgrace, I listen to my loved ones mourn, feeling my heart broken and torn, now I am in these brick walls, trying to stay strong, fighting all the urges to end it all, but I keep my head up high, realize I have a family out there that cares, so whatever this place got to throw at me, I have to take a deep breath, look it in the eyes, and say, "Give me your best shot!" and 'til I come home, for all my loved ones out there waiting for me, I may be away, but I am never gone. . ..

HOME

Brittney

I'm coming home,
I'm breaking from this dome
this devil will not
make me a rebel anymore.

I'm free
I'm going on a spree,
to be out of this cage
I can let go
of all this rage.

I'm not going to daze
in this maze
but I am amazed.

THE FEELING

Brittney

You will remember
how it felt
where you dealt
with what you hated
this time it was a blessing
and a lesson learned

You will remember me.

The walls—
where no one bawls
for these calls—

in this cell
where I dwell.

You'll remember that face
when they told you
you were going to that place.

That time was like never
and like always,
I always dreaded ending
up here, I had to face it.

I came in with nothing;
I will leave with something.

GUIDE ME TO THE RIGHT PATH—I

Robert

Today on this beautiful day in such a dark place I lay. I lay thinking to myself of all the dark things and people that surround me in this place perceived as hell and still somehow I could see the light. What does this mean? It's this light that gives me hope, strengthens my faith, and allows me to believe that no matter what obstacle shall be put in my way though out life meant to test me to see if I am worthy enough to achieve greatness. I shall and will overcome because I am great, and capable of great things; like the light that is perpetual to these dark walls that are sealed with pain, sorrow, and loneliness, blood, sweat, and tears. This light that gives hope to the ones that need it most. And, I shall do the same when I finally emerge from this dark place they call hell, into a new life with everlasting light and uncontrollable opportunities for achieving greatness and give hope to the people that are stuck on this broken path, and show them the light.

GUIDE ME TO THE RIGHT PATH—II

Robert

Today mixed emotions flood my mind and overwhelm my soul with waves of doubt. It reminds me of my internal threats. My fingers felt this once before, trial of emotions slayed across paper, it proposed run on sentences, the heart you once felt is abolished in a hole of pain. This concrete destiny has sealed my nerves filled with senseless feelings. Scared of what is next for me but trying to stay positive cause failure is not an option for me. Need to stay strong for the ones that love me, myself and my God, for I am worthy of achieving greatness. Knowing my God will never steer me wrongfully. What is in store for me is a blessing, a second chance, a new way of life, and the first step of being able to achieve the greatness that I am more than capable of achieving. Knowing this I shall fear no more, my mind at ease. And, my soul lifted from this pit of doubt and destruction. My demands that follow me will no longer be a threat to me, cause I am reborn, today I am a new man with a new way of life and as long as I follow this way I have nothing to fear.

FROM PRISON TO THE STREETS

Misty

From prison to the street
My head needs to meet my feet

No place to go, don't know where
My next meal will be

This freedom I craved seems completely
New to me

Familiar faces fade to only enemies
I have lost all my trust

Within I no longer feel confident
It's all been replaced with self-disgust

From prison to the street
Worse than before my head isn't
even with my feet

All the ideas and the false laid
plans have fallen through

Not even sure where to go
or what to even do

Not a dollar in my pocket
and nothing to my name

The harsh realization that I
am the only one to blame.

From prison to the street
My head needs to meet my feet

Feeling lower than the dirt
beneath my shoes

it washes over me so quickly
the all to familiar blues

Starting from the bottom
the top is out of sight

The urge to get high is
going to be the hardest fight

From prison to the street
My head needs to meet my feet.

THE NIGHT SKY

Nikkole

> The moon, the stars, and the planets.
> What looks like it could be a world away,
> we are just fortunate enough to behold.
> The colors, the lights, the sparkles and its shine.
> Illuminating things within our galaxy
> that could steal the breath from under
> the most guarded man's hold.
> Clusters of dust and life.
> Things we can only dream of,
> for they are so gracious and out of reach.
> Laying in the green pastures of this earth,
> awestruck at such an adoring sight.
> The moon, the stars, and the planets.
> What looks like it could be a world away,
> we are just fortunate enough to behold.

WHY SHOULD LEAVING HERE SCARE ME

Nikkole

As a small child
I can't remember moments of time
when every risk taking decision
was anyone else's but mine.
While being told to be cautious,
to watch my every step
The boundaries I was given
were never very well kept.
Ironic enough, captivity
opens quite a few doors
Ones that otherwise would have remained
unnoticed and ignored.
The memories you start creating
become happy and benign.
All of the troubles and the trauma
you learn to get passed and leave behind.
The people I have met from every walk of life
Remind me that no matter who you are
we all come with some pain and strife.
The memories I have made here
unable to compare
And isn't that one of the best reasons
to have a scare?
Because outside of these walls
anything could be there.

LOSING MYSELF

Antoinette

> So far away
> longing to smell their hair
> touch their cheeks
> Just look how beautiful
> my babies are
> Longing to pull their
> covers up to their chin
> to give them a kiss
> and say goodnight.
> Wanting to be there if they
> wake with a bad dream
> Long to hear
> those beautiful words;
> RFJ.

STARTING OVER

Antoinette

> I sit and think of
> the things that
> are in my head.
> The past, the things
> I have done.
> The hurt I have caused.
> The promises I have broken.
> When is it enough.
> I sit here broken
> wishing to start over.
> Finally, having
> a second chance.
> No more mistakes.
> No regrets.
> Ready to live.

THE LEAVES

Antoinette

> The leaves fall off the trees.
> I rake them into a pile.
> Just for the wind
> to blow them away.
> Losing myself with
> the sorrow of the storm
> in my heart, wondering if I
> will ever see
> the sun through the storm.

TO BE YOUNG

Antoinette

> To be young again,
> in a yard that you loved
> that takes you back to being young
> feeding the ducks and watching
> the geese fly away.
> A place that you felt safe
> that is now far away.
> How you wish just
> one more day.

YOUR TURN

Melissa

> The darkest place I have ever been
> is inside my own mind.
> It has tortured me, made me believe
> I wasn't worth the life.
> I've talked down to myself
> and bled at my own hand.
> I have sabotaged my own body,
> my happiness, my life.
> I thought I had overcome
> these things, but have I really.
> I think I have only found
> someone to do it for me,
> someone else to blame for my pain.
> Now you sabotage everything
> for us and torture my mind.
> Some how it only hurts
> so much more.
> Now you're the things I
> love and hate the most.
> The only one who can hurt
> me is me, and I do.
> I hurt myself with you.

TRACY SPADE

Melissa

Another day in jail and there's nothing much to do.
"Please make this day go faster," I pray.
My mind is going crazy with another boring day.
So I sit next to the "Queen of Spades".

She asks me to sit in and I say, "I don't know how".
She says, "Honey you're going to learn today".
Cards are flying fast but she remembers what's been played.
That's why they call her the Queen of Spades.

"Just follow suit, try to beat what's thrown,
Don't be nervous it's just a game.
I'll teach you to play like me, then we're gonna own.
You're learning from the Queen of Spades."

I catch on really quickly and I'm gaining confidence.
We've been playing all day, everyday.
Now we're spanking all these b——-s and we win
the tournament because my partner is the Queen of Spades.

Now today is her max, and I'm really gonna miss her
But nobody ever wants to stay.
So today she left and I hugged her and I kissed her,
And now I am the Queen of Spades.

REGRETS

Stacey

> Watching tree limbs swaying in the breeze
> Seeing patches of yard that will never again be green
> The ideas and the memories of how we used to play
> Oh how easily we gave them away.

MY MICHAEL

Stacey

You're my heart, my soul, my love, my light
I cherish every bit of you with all my might
I grip every moment with you so very tight
No one can ever take this away as my right
For my desire for you is my strongest plight
And, forever with you is something I will never fight.

ALSO FOR MICHAEL

S̲t̲acey

> When I finally get to hug you again, you better never let me go. I am not one to cry but that voice of yours is going to go right through me. There is nothing that will be able to wipe the smile off my face. For there is nothing in this world I am looking forward to more because forever and a day with you will never ever be nearly enough.

LIFE AS A BUTCHER'S DAUGHTER

Stacey

Animals frozen in a tomb of ice
the arrows still in place from when it took their life
Watching a man work wayside his wife
surrounded by the glint and gleam of every knife
The sinks never stay empty
All the ovens steadily going
The overpowering stench of freshly sawed bone
Dear God, someone please answer that phone!
The endless piles of garbage
The never ending duties of clean up
My dad, the butcher, his life is a constant bustle
but hey, every man has to have his own hustle!

FREEDOM

Stacey

> I sit alone behind the wheel of my convertible
> so many birds engulfing me in their songs
> I crave the fresh air that blasts against me
> My happiness is here in the endless open blue
> skies that surround me.

THE RIGHT AMOUNT OF WRONG

Stacey

It stemmed from a friend's persistence
She was determined to set me up
She made me choose from a line
Told me to "suck it up, buttercup"
When I made my choice
her man said, "not the f——today!"
He's not the one for you
so he pushed his friend my way
We started to talk
Just a little here and there
Who this guy was I was completely unaware
He's not afraid to come back at me
cuz God knows I always have something to say
And even though he keeps me on my toes
I tell him "Boy you gonna learn today"
He's on point in his mindset
I think he's on my same page
He makes me laugh with his wit
So for now he's got center stage
We end up with a lot in common
his rap hits the beat of my song
And although he wasn't the one I chose
he's turned out to be just the right
amount of wrong.

FAST LIFE

STACEY

> I love and live for the thrill of the fast life
> the intensity, the excitement, the momentum
> I've moved through these streets on my own for so long
> Living life for nothing but the next high, that
> the next challenge, that next dollar.
> Never expecting to come across someone who
> can keep up with the rhythm I've set
> someone who fills my heart
> someone who matches my mind
> but every queen does deserve a king by her side
> we run fast, we stay constant, we play even
> harder, we barely left any time for just one another.
> One day they kicked in his door, held him to the
> ground, ripped through his house.
> They inevitably took him away from me.
> My love, my light, my life now gone
> my everything taken out of my sight.
> However I think I am strong, no tears fall from these
> eyes. I continue to cover our hustle
> I handle the pace for us both
> No time to feel, too high to cry, too much pride
> to even wanna try.
> A few weeks go past, the dust begins to settle,
> the drugs have finally worn off
> I feel the sadness, the emptiness in my heart now crushing
> A random song comes on the radio, the flood gates
> open, my mind and soul finally break.
> Only then came forth the endless stream of tears and
> I promise I'll hold true to you throughout
> these next two years.

MY OWN PRISON

Amy

My prison began at sixteen,
on my own, young,
scared, innocent
men older men
they knew better
didn't they?
they kept me safe
took care of me,
but at what cost?
drugs, guns, blades, fights,
many come and go
death so much death I see
too much, saw too much, did
too much, got out now and
I am married and started
a new life, a new game, my game
my hustle, yet still in my own prison
in ways no one knows.

Then I got careless
caught charges doing
a bid, will this get me out?
No. Cause my prison is my life.
I choose to hustle, bustle,
steal and deal. I choose this. It's
up to me to open those gates
and walk out and be free, so can I?
Of course I can but I will I? Probably
not. The game sucks you in sometimes,
there is no out, this is my prison. I can

only fix for now. I am good at this, it won't
let me out, he won't let me out. So, this
is my dark-side, my prison. One day it will
stop. 'Til then, here I am destroying people
and myself, but it pays the bills. They
taught me the game but forgot to say
it will never stop once you are in.
That's it. Welcome to my life, my prison.

MY SECOND CHANCE

Amy

Jail my salvation
Addiction my torturer
the pain I feel with it
the pain I feel without it
the sirens in the distance
the runners warning that they are coming
we scatter like roaches
the smell of drugs make me sweat
make me itch
almost died more times
than I can tell you
came to jail now I am sober
now my heads clear and I feel pain
again this is my second chance of nine
don't matter it's my chance to live again
so Jail my salvation
Addiction my torturer
jail saved me in more ways
than you know so now
I torture myself to fight the addiction
so right now as I sit in jail
I am safe
this is my salvation.

WEEPING WILLOW

Amy

Weeping Willow with your branches
hanging down, why do you make me frown?
Was it because he allowed himself
to be taken away? Or, because he wouldn't stay?
Another great man taken away too soon,
my heart is shattered it hurts so much. Is it greedy
to have wanted to keep him? I didn't get to
say good-bye because I am stuck here
in this cell. I am stuck in
my own personal hell. His funeral was planned
from a payphone in jail with no one but
myself to cry to. Is this my punishment
for all I have done? Why was it his time
he was so young? Why couldn't it have
been another way. The needle came in between us
like so many times before. Just this time you
took too much. No thoughts of me or
anyone else at all. Just sitting here
blaming myself with no shit to do
but think of you. I'll spread your
ashes around our tree, our time together
was too short, but one hell of a journey. My sweet
Weeping Willow with your branches hanging down,
when my time comes I will join you
but until then, rest your head
my dear sweet friend.

ONE LONELY ANGEL

Delta

An icy blade cuts through my skin
A red river flows off my finger tips
Dizziness takes over, day turns to night
as I fall into an endless sleep
Every thought I had, every memory I knew
Swelled up into smoke, all the tears are nowhere near.
Flying high through the sky, looking down onto you
Why cry now? Why act like you care?
You were never there
when I cried for help, when I cried through the pain.
Thick fog surrounds me as the years pass by
no more tears when you come to say goodbye.
I rise above my stone as I fly off alone
Young in a world of lies is nothing more than
a dark nightmare within my mind.

MASK OF THE NIGHT

Delta

The nights are colder but the stars still shine bright
a yellow and orange glow dance through the night
The memories of us was a life filled with green like what the leaves
use to be is now a dreaded orangish, brown beneath my feet,
with each step I take a million pieces break away running through
the night trying to escape the howling of the wolves
Breaking into tears as it turns into the sound of your voice
the time of year that use to smell like apple pie, maple treats,
and pumpkin spice. Now becomes a scent of dying love.
The time of year I used to love is now a nightmare
I wish to run from, I hide in the night
no more yellow and orange glow to be my light
You don't need a mask to walk through the night.

MY SAFE HOME

Delta

> The rock home where I run to hides as far back as I can go, with the coldness of the stones traveling through my toes. Overlooking the river below as I sit alone listening to my faded cries as if plays fresh before my eyes. The evergreen fills the air bringing me to a place where I won't be scared.

AWAY FROM HOME

Ashley

> Unfamiliar faces all around
> Bodies dressed in the same attire.
> Off to medical we go
> Hurry up and wait
> You may miss a show.
>
> Voices screaming all around me,
> As they take me somewhere
> That doesn't ground me.
> I had everything I desire,
> But I messed it all up for you.
>
> Went to a new place so I could see
> That, that life wasn't for me.
> You weren't meant for me,
> Nor was I meant for you.
> I saw where this was going to go.
>
> I worked hard for where I got.
> But an awful hard lesson I was taught.
> Discharged and left for the first plane home,
> Ended up with a heart of stone.
>
> Baby boy just three months old
> Being raised to a broken home.
> His mom fought up to divorce.
> Hidden affairs leading to bitterness.
> Leads me to nothing but life's a mess.
>
> Time behind bars,
> Nothing false is true.

Can't wait to leave here
To be somewhere new.
Maybe even be with someone new.

I should have stayed at that place
Away From Home.

NOWHERE

Ashley

Just like time
My anxiety stricken mind won't stop.
Always needing a quick getaway.
To console every part of me that hurts.
I take a walk to what I call now,
Nowhere.
Down the neighborhood street
Was a little turnaround paved with dirt,
Out of breath I think, "Isn't this redundant?"
"How is this relaxing?"
Walk over to a hidden dirt and rock path,
Hidden by all the trees.
I hear running water as I get near,
I see something that looks like paradise.
There was a creek with water running slow,
And trees blocking every view.
Sunshine glistening off the water,
And boulders stuck in the dirty sand.
I could just sit for hours,
Clearing my stress ridden heart and mind.
A few years after my accidental discovery,
Hurricane Sandy hit and washed it away.
My safe place was left barren,
Turned into a boulder wall.
I've found other spots to go,
But nothing can compare
To my place I call
Nowhere.

I NEED YOU TO KNOW

Ashley

I needed you to know
How I feel inside.
I needed you to know
That I mean no harm.

We may be complete strangers
But I can see who you are.
All you have to do is look at me
And I can see the safety inside.

I needed you to know
I'll be here if you need me
Simply because I want to.
I just need you to see me.

I needed you to know
I see those beautiful eyes.
And every look you give me,
Makes me nervous inside.

I needed you to know
I don't need you.
If you don't need me,
We could separate easy.

I'd leave my past all behind
To start over brand new.
That's a sacrifice I'd make for you.
I just needed you to know.

SITTING IN THE YARD

Dorothy

>Sitting in the yard
watching the other inmates
walk, talk, and play sports.
Sitting in the yard
watching the cars and trucks
go by.
Sitting in the yard
waiting to hear the whistle
of the fire sirens.
Sitting in the yard
I am slowly dreading
getting in trouble.
Sitting in the yard
by myself is
sad and depressing.

SUMMER TO FALL

Dorothy

    The end of summer is the beginning of fall
    When the summer air begins to cool
    Raking leaves and picking up sticks
    Watching the sky go from light to dark
    Watching scary movies
    Going to haunted houses
    And taking my haunted hay rides
    to get to the corn mazes
    is so fun and amazing.

PUMPKIN PICKING

Dorothy

>Picking pumpkins to paint with the little ones
>Decorating and dressing up for Halloween
>Being invited to many Halloween parties,
>finding what costume to wear to each one
>Running over the crunching leaves
>Going house to house, saying trick or treat
>In your scary or funny costumes getting candy
>Getting home, eating pumpkin or apple pie, drinking
>pumpkin spice coffee or tea.

IN THE SHOP

Dorothy

    Standing here in the shop
    Listening to music and hearing the shop phones ring
    waiting on a car to come through the garage doors.
    Getting the car ready for an inspection
    Putting it on a lift, lifting it up
    Looking at the underside of the motor
    Starting an oil change, changing the filter, draining the oil
    Oil running down my arms
    Lowering the lift, putting new oil in
    Smelling gas or antifreeze from any leaky lines
    Checking the brake lines to make sure they are not leaking
    Grease on my face, clothes covered in grease and oil
    Smelling like gas.

UNVEILED

Dorothy

> When I see her, I see need
> I see a black gift wrapped in pink paper
> I see a skeleton draped in red velvet
> I see a frown hiding in a smile
> I see filth and dirt covered by a rose garden

WHAT IS LOVE

Dorothy

What the f— is love anyway?
Is it a phone call the next morning?
Is it picking up a hundred dollar meal tab?
Is it flowers on the fifth date?
Or is it sleeping on the wet spot?

You are wrong to think I have no feelings,
You are wrong to think I would not care,
You are not sorry so don't tell me you are,
You are nothing to me, just some distant black star.

FAULT

Dorothy

    I have no one but myself to blame
    This is all my fault
    It hurts
    It will always hurt
    I will never forget
    I could try and I will try but I will never forget
    It will burn in my memory forever
    Just like everything else
    I will not be able to put this away.

REET'S PLACE

Kristen

    Sunlight shining on
    A Garden Goddess tanning
    The shadow of Rita's Peace Pole
    telling its own time
    Gladiolas leaning on
    Peace and beauty
    in Unity.

GRAMMY'S HOUSE

Kristen

> That little cottage
> halfway up the hill
> Papa built lovingly for her
> stone by stone
> Each hand picked
> from the babbling creek below
> The bed in our playroom
> never really slept in
> Covered in her crazy 60's
> patchwork quilt
> Pinks and blues and reds and yellows
> Many afternoons I spent reading
> that big pile of Nancy Drew
> kept full of unread volumes
> She made sure I could check off
> everyone as I read
> And still the smell of blackberry jam
> Grammy would have bubbling away
> and sealing in jars with wax on top
> Will always leave me yearning
> tears in my eyes
> for her and her house
> my safest place—
> Home.

SAX FREEDOM

Kristen

>Subway doors open—
>An Exodus—
>with the cacophony of the masses
>Offensive subway station smells
>sights and sounds
>Assault the sense
>Village Jazz Clubs swell
>with the sax man's freedom wail.

THE TOO MANY AIRPORT HEARTBREAK

KRISTEN

>In a New York airport
>That first day Adam left me
>Berlin Bound—
>Electric Bass in hand
>My Jazz Man and I
>Never notice any Airport Bustle
>Lost in saying. . .
>Goodbye
>Then
>Airport after Airport
>Europe to New York
>Joyful Heartbreak
>Hello
>Then—
>Always saying
>Goodbye.

TIME

Kristen

> I have nothing but time?
> When?
> Religion, Poetry, Laundry, 12 Steps
> Serious "I" work in progress
> There is no time
> For full days, morning to night
> There is no rest for this wicked one
> Swiftly this time goes by
> Life is Chaos and
> There is no Time.

ALL THE STRETCH MARKS OF MY LIFE

Kristen

All of these lines
Shiny and spidery
Running up and down
Crisscrossing over themselves
My symbolic scars of motherhood
Proving my growth of another being
Giving new life to my love
Telling the story of that love
Pure and Primal in its growth
My Mother's Badge
of the circle of life
Marking and making me
mom and proud.

SERIOUSLY, FORGIVENESS?

Kristen

> I'm pissed off
> I must write a poem
> A poem about forgiveness
> Forgiving myself
> What?
> Here? Now?
> In this God forsaken place?
> With these bars and clanging keys?
> There is no forgiveness here
> They don't allow it
> Punishment—
> That's this game
> Humanity? Humility?
> Forget it!
> They don't sell that here
> Last names and numbers
> That's all you are
> Self worth? Self Identity? Self love?
> Leave that at the metal door
> There is no one here to write a poem.

Tom's Poems

SLOWLY SINKING RIDGES—WRITTEN AT THE PRISON

The slowly sinking ridges of
the far-off mountain gap
drawl me all along their edges
to the fields of random
bushes, brush, and trees
below.
To the creek,
to the creek at the bottom
at the bottom
of the purpling clumps of brambles.

There is a cunning that
comes from being able
to survive out there—
out there against all
of the odds of the
things my insides would
have me to do.
A cunning that knows
just what wood I should
gather for my fire;
just what branches I need
to start it;
so I may
ease into the
gentle wholeness it calls
out of me. The wholeness
of men, and trails, and woods,
and all of the odds it takes to
survive. The wholeness
of things my crimes would

not be able to call forth
out of my depths.

How to burn despair
into the ash of hope;
how to weave anger
into learning to stay
alive; how to turn a whim
into patience and no act
that would harm my chance
at being free.

There is a cunning in
tending to the deeper
pieces of my me; one
that sets me to thrive
and not just simply
to survive with that
impulse to have.

And so,
I climb atop the
hill that possesses me,
to the mountaintop that
gives me view of
all that is spread so
gently all around.
And, from this vantage point
I ask myself, "Do I have
what I need within my
soul? What I need
to make my way through
all I see out there?"

HIDDEN

A stillness
lies hidden
just beyond the
beyond.

A step further than
you feel like you
can drag yourself
along.

You must push
yourself through
to the other side,
but it is
there—

always there.

Waiting for you
to enter.

And,
you do not.

Just because
you hear the locking
of the door—

behind you
as you leave
the prison walls—
does not mean

that you
are

free.

Enter
the stillness
spread out

in front of you
and all
around—

EVERYWHERE.

Then,
you can
cry

FREE.

MY EYES ARE FALLING

I could die
a good man;

if I could
pass while
my eyes are

falling on trees
of color—

trees of Autumn.
Maybe—

if I could
speak slowly
enough;

perhaps one word
drawn out
over a million
years

I could enter
these mountains
gradually over
time;

a bit here and
there amid the
aching hours
of their
rising and
creation.

Maybe
that would be
the way to go.

Drained back
into all that is
around us

one electron
at a time.

THE AROMA OF A WORD

The aroma of a word
has caught itself in
the back of my throat;

so I can both
taste and smell its
delight and impact
all at once.

It smells
and tastes
of ginseng.

It lingers there—
a fragrance seeking
respite and

germination;

a planting of
its tuberous meaning
and earthy hints toward
complexity

in something I shall
call for now—
a soul.

How might I
tend it to fullness,

that it may rise and
murmur its very longing
and desire;

a sound to set us free
from a stifling oppression—

a croak to release us
from a kind of silence
that is soaking wet
with anger and remonstration.

That word
has found itself
mingling in my mouth
and waiting

itself to be born.

We must wake up
to the aroma of the sounds
that are building;

without them, we might
never find our way back
to what it means to be

human.

STAND OUT AMONG THE WINDS

Stand out—
you mouth breather—

stand out among the
mighty winds and
glorious droplets of
cold winter rain;

and look up.

Close your eyes

and breathe in.
Breathe in deeply—

through your nose.

Feel the splashes of
cold wetness on your
forearms and on

your face.

Hear what escapes our
listening while we work;

the majestic gusts of air
that seem to howl around
and up; back to the skies.

Don't ever forget this;
for this is what is real.
Stand firmly upon both
feet and soak up all that

can be known with every
cell your body avails.

You are awash with the
wonder of quarks; you are
replete with the amazement of
quasars. It only takes
one atom to be broken
open to awe to set the
universe aflame. Find that
pearl, clasp that ducat.

Sell all you have
for that one electron

to SEE!

THE VOICES

It does not take much
for me to be able
to hear the trailing
off sentences and
artful conversation of
the physicians on
the porch of this
abandoned hospital
where men and women
were discarded for the
inappropriateness of
their ideas and emotion.
The way they spoke
or lurched and craned
their necks—this way and
that—offended those
just over the wall out
there—along the edges
of the property—covered
with razor wire and
barbed wire to maim
their already stifled
bodies and wounded
souls. They were regarded
as no more than dilapidated
specimens of mankind
gone awry and
just plain mad.

The cadence of their madness in drastic contradistinction to the world we have convinced ourselves we must possess at all costs.

SOME DAYS

Awaken.

Awaken if you

can from your own

self made drama of

things you have seen to

be the most important

things in

the world.

And,

look around you at

all of those who are

dying too young;

leaving before

they have tasted

the white peach in summer,

the avocado just ripened

this moment, the

day lily bulb sautéed

in butter and sea salt.

There is one here

that just became a father,

and one there that

has just born a child.

This small baby has

just learned to breathe

without a machine,

and that child there

has finally laid down to

sleep—starving—in

a field of dead crops.

Is the rancor that you

have allowed to swallow you

so undoable that you

cannot smell the milkweed

blossoms as they invade

the machinations of your

soul that is trapped on

the treadmill you have

built yourself.

Awaken, myself.

Awaken.

Some days the

flash of truth can

light up my mind

and I can see

for a moment

everything as it is,

lightening revealing

the true lay of

the land.

Awaken myself.

Awaken.

CREATING A SELF

The mystics
have often called it
the self-project—

the ego-project—

the project
of building an
image that we
can love
and adore

of ourselves.

Just shy of
worship.

Making ourselves
our self

that we can tolerate

or, learn

at least

to live with.

I would like
to appear pious,
or patient or astute

and filled with infinite
wisdom from the dawn
of time.

Expecting that there
is a core in there that
is stable and changes
not.

The I cannot
believe elsewise.

But,
what if the
thing

that remains
is always new.

But who is
the one inside

that gets to say

"I" do not
like who "I"

have become. "I"
need to change

that "I".

Who is it
that is

uncomfortable as

I watch my I become

more me.

That one,

needs a vacation.

SILENCE LIKE DEW

There is a stillness
that is beyond wonder
and awe.

It is beyond
the beyond of all
things.

It is in that place
the heart longs
to repose—

even if for but
a moment. The
place where silence
runs stronger than
a meandering river.

The whisper of
a blade of grass in
the morning breeze
can take you there;

the grandeur of
Half-Dome at sunset
can reveal the way.

Whether by the smallest
of the small, or by the
greatest of the great;

go into that space and
find yourself a home.

It is there that
all things converge;

it is there that the
confluence of everything
rises into itself anew—
reborn.

Find that space
no matter the cost.
There, the silence is
so loud it loses
all focus and becomes
a glistening dew
on Indra's grand net
of awareness. All
things become
new again.

And again.

WHERE IT LAY

Poetry.
It lay
just beyond the
murky, silent (whole)
confluence of being.
It appears and resides
as an image, and then
a word.

Poetry is born,
thus—
out of pure, raw being,
and not experience.
For, experience must always
arise after image;
after word.

It is the lapping noise
of the ocean on the sand,
on the rocks along the
coast of coldness and
of warmth.
It is the trailing
vapor of a cloud
as it leaves itself
to shift itself
in mist or rain, in
forms and torrents.

Always out from
and just before it
happens itself

into an experience.

There is the vital power
of the word upon
the soul and sound
upon the heart.

Born at once
with utterance and
sight. But
always roiling
at a slow boil from
the murky, silent (whole)
confluence of being.

Always to

become.

I LOOK TO THE HILLS

There is never any
doubt where my eyes
will look in this
idyllic landscape
of our home.

To the hills,
always to the hills
do I lift up my eyes;

I look to the hills.

Most times it is
an autonomic response
to my panning
across the horizon,

watchful and attentive
as a wonder-seeker,

an awe-junkie.
Trees call me to their
leaves or hollow absence
of the same;

pointing up

across the treetops
our hungry vision
is lured up, always up
toward the places in which
the landscape is pushed
heavenward by unseen

and colossal tectonic machinations.

Mountains, hills,
bluffs and ridges
pull our sight up them in
a backward alluviation of
fallen debris.

I look to the hills
and am lost in a
whirring noise
that is the backdrop
of all space and time.

Radical amazement has
come into me from what
these eyes have seen.

I behold glory in a
pile of earth, I feel
mystery in the tremendum
of these mountains,
I smell humility in the
dirt of these hills.

I look to the hills

and let the stillness in.

LINGERING—FOR MICHAEL AND HIS FAMILY

You could tell
it was the fading
of the milkweed
blossoms

—those
fair and tender
blooms of the roadsides
and the fields.

Their scent
a lingering of
phlox and lilac;

hints of verbena
in the cool.

Their aroma mingles
strongly

and hangs
heavy

in both
the morning
and the evening
air.

How is it we cannot
describe a thing without
the using of another thing;

in a short or long chain of

descriptive words and
similes.

How might we say a life
without other lives to
spread the meaning out
before us in landscapes of
like and as.

Shades of purpling
pink and dusty roads
are vibrant in the softly
closing time and
hues of their
hiatus.

As they stand
there

on their stalks,

in the mingled earth
of all that has
come before

they are nothing
without the nutrients
of the past
soaking into them—

history matters.
Our lives and
theirs are nothing

more than

a giving over of
an aroma that is

part ours and part from
our people—from all
that have come before

It passes on

—through us—

like their scent

in this
cool breeze.

It lands upon
the lives of
all around

giving pause

a chance to smile
and to feel the special
inkling

that can only come
in a realization.

I love that smell.
I love that sight.
What can we not
gain from

their simple being.

We are this,

pieces of all that
have come before

given over to us
for this moment

and then,

then we are

theirs. Carried
away

gently on the
tendrils
and tiny feet
of those

who have
sought to

gain from us—

one cool
draught;

an aroma
of majestic
sweetness

but only so
an hour.

A FADING FULL-MOON

It is a morning
for Chicory flowers,
Queen Anne's Lace,
and a silent, waning
full-moon.

They were all
just right there,
at my side
and straight ahead.

Honest ignorance
about something said
but not known.

That is all my
words can be when
I bring up the
beauty I see.

For I have not
written
these things into being;

I have only written
their written-ness
into verse. Very
different.

The handiwork
that is written into all
creation comes from

a far more gifted hand;

a more robust tongue
crafts and gilds those
words. Mine is the

pleasure to simply
point to them and say,

"ah, such glory."

OX-BOW LAKE

This oxbow lake
of midlife is cut
off from
the full meander of
my days across this
earth-place.

Nutrients remain.
Gathered
from the countless
sloughing-offs of
their origins
far and away
in the collected-ness of
who I have been.

A childhood
memory of learning
to write my name
on the back of a
double blue card
from Candyland
having seeped into
the rock over which the
streaming of my pieces
have flowed. An amble
along the cornfield
in the mid-winter
morning of my high school
days of trapping
is drawn up into the
tree trunk that sits

just at the water's edge.

But the whole of the water
is left to less than
it has been
by the rushing flood
of constant change
calling me away
from the well worn
bed of my days.

There is a circuitousness
to the love between geology
and our souls. A way
we come full round to seeing
what and where we have been
and how we have become.

What moves beyond
and what remains
has been a question
that is given up
over and over throughout
the lives of humankind.

A flood pushes through
a sidewinding branch,
carving new routines
into the foundation of
our bedrock. A handful
of things are left here,
but most are gone.

Who is the who
that is left behind?
A leaf floats across
the surface of the
river and is lodged
along the red clay
silt packed together
as a berm on the edges
of this water-course.
Tomorrow it shall
become dirt, too.

Who is the who
that determines meaning
as we shift and change
and idle in our banks
of the water of our days?

This oxbow lake
of midlife is cut
off from
the full meander of
my days across this
earth-place.

Nutrients remain.
Gathered
from the countless
sloughing-offs of
their origins
far and away
in the collected-ness of
who I have been.

www.ingramcontent.com/pod-product-compliance
Lightning Source LLC
Chambersburg PA
CBHW070248100426
42743CB00011B/2181